iScience
Readers

Water:
Watch It Change

by Emily Sohn and Laura Townsend

Chief Content Consultant
Edward Rock
Associate Executive Director, National Science Teachers Association

NORWOOD HOUSE PRESS
Chicago, Illinois

Norwood House Press
PO Box 316598
Chicago, IL 60631

For information regarding Norwood House Press, please visit our website at
www.norwoodhousepress.com or call 866-565-2900.

Special thanks to: Amanda Jones, Amy Karasick, Alanna Mertens, Terrence Young, Jr.

photos on page 27 courtesy of U.S. Geological Survey, Department of the Interior/USGS

Editors: Barbara J. Foster, Diane Hinckley
Designer: Daniel M. Greene
Production Management: Victory Productions, Inc.

Library of Congress Cataloging-in-Publication Data

Sohn, Emily.

Water: watch it change / by Emily Sohn and Laura Townsend.
p. cm.—(Iscience readers)

Summary: "Describes the multitude of ways water affects our lives, and
shows that water can change forms like a superhero. As readers use scientific
inquiry to learn about all of the different things water can do and be, an
activity based on real world situations challenges them to apply what they've
learned in order to solve a puzzle"—Provided by publisher.

Includes bibliographical references and indexes.

ISBN-13: 978-1-59953-422-0 (library edition: alk. paper)
ISBN-10: 1-59953-422-3 (library edition: alk. paper)

1. Water—Juvenile literature. I. Townsend, Laura. II. Title.

QC145.24.S64 2011
546'.22—dc22
2010044544

CONTENTS

Note to Caregivers:

Throughout this book, many questions are posed to the reader. Some are open-ended and ask what the reader thinks. Discuss these questions with your child and guide him or her in thinking through the possible answers and outcomes. There are also questions posed which have a specific answer. Encourage your child to read through the text to determine the correct answer. Most importantly, encourage answers grounded in reality while also allowing imaginations to soar. Information to help support you as you share the book with your child is provided in the back in the **Additional Notes** section.

Words that are **bolded** are defined in the glossary in the back of the book.

The Amazing Powers of Water

Water is everywhere. We use it every day. We drink it. We take baths in it. We cook with it. Water keeps us alive. Water can also change form and make other things change as well. What happens when you heat it, cool it, or stir something into it?

In this book you will learn about all the fun things water can do. It seems like magic, but it's science!

Where Does Water on the Outside of a Glass Come From?

Jack, age 7, sits down for lunch on a hot summer day. He has a sandwich and an apple. Best of all, he has a fresh glass of ice water. He is just about to take a big gulp. Then he sees it: There is water on the outside of the glass. But, wait! That water hadn't been there just a minute ago. How did the glass get wet on the outside?

Jack doesn't know how water got on the outside of his glass. Can you help him solve the mystery?

Is the glass leaking or is something else happening? What do you think? After reading this book, you might change your mind.

Like Jack, you can do an experiment with water. (You may need to ask for help.) Put two glasses on a table. Fill them halfway with water that is about the same temperature as the air in the room.

When you choose two glasses, be sure they are identical.

Put ice in one of the glasses. Which glass do you think will form water on the outside? Wait ten minutes. Now look. Write down what you see.

Watching Water Change

Water is like a magician. Kazam! Sometimes it just disappears! This is easy to understand once you know the science behind it. Here's an activity you can try with the help of an adult.

Put one cup of water in a pot. Put the pot on a hot stove. Watch as bubbles form. That means the water is **boiling.**

If you wait long enough, the water will disappear from the pot. Where did the water go?

What happens as a pot of water boils and boils?

It may look like magic, but there's science going on. When water boils, it turns to steam. Water is a **liquid.** Steam is a **gas.** Water and steam are two different forms of the exact same thing.

How is water different as a liquid and a gas? How did the water appear on Jack's glass? How did it disappear from the pot? Read on to find out.

What Are the Three States of Water?

Water, ice, and steam. Are they really all the same thing?

Under the right conditions, water can change from one form to another. And every time it changes, it has different "powers," called properties in science.

You've already seen how water can be a liquid sometimes and a gas other times. It can also be a **solid.** You know the solid as ice. Let's explore the three states of water. Along the way, we'll discover how water changes from one state to another. We'll also see some of water's other special properties.

Water takes up more space as it freezes. These icebergs formed and piled up as ocean water froze.

What Happens When Water Freezes?

Under cold temperatures, water **molecules** slow down. As they freeze, they spread out. Imagine a game of freeze-tag. All the molecules move away from each other. Then they stop. Just like that, water expands as it freezes.

What would happen if you filled a plastic bottle with water and put it in the freezer? Get an adult's help. Then try it and see.

In its liquid state, water can be quite refreshing!

Imagine a huge swimming pool. How would you turn all that water into a solid? Simple: Just make it cold—very cold.

When the temperature gets low enough, liquid water will start **freezing** and change into solid ice. So now the pool is a skating rink. How can you unfreeze it? Just add heat. Ta-da! The water is liquid again.

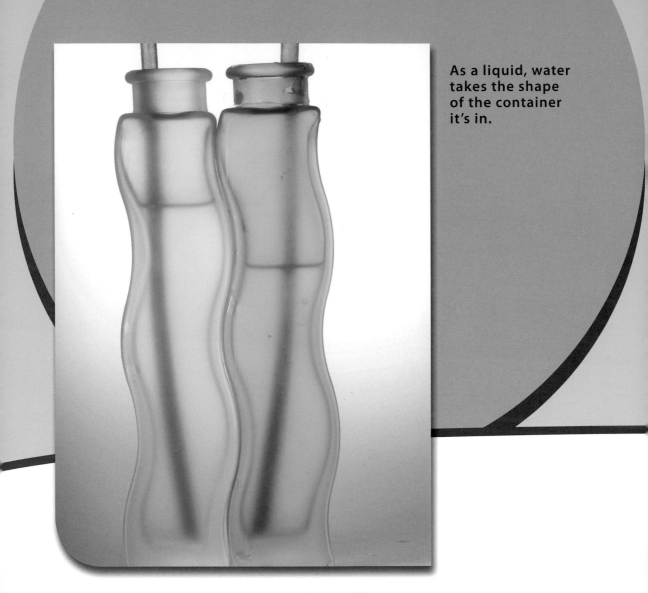

As a liquid, water takes the shape of the container it's in.

Can Water Change Shape?

As you grow, your body changes shape. Water can do better than that. When water is a liquid, it takes the shape of whatever container it is in. Pick a container. A square vase. A round pot. A snowman cake pan. You name the container and water will slosh around to follow the shape.

How Does Water Become a Gas?

Remember the pot of water that boiled away? Heat explains that "trick." Just by getting hot, liquid water became an invisible gas.

As the molecules move faster, they move farther away from each other and some escape the liquid altogether.

As water gets hotter and hotter, molecules in the water start moving faster and faster. The more these tiny particles move, the more they bump into each other. It's kind of like a big dance party right in your kitchen.

With all that jumping and jostling, some molecules break free from their liquid form. They turn into gas and become **water vapor.** Presto! The water has disappeared.

13

Now You See It, Now You Don't

You don't need a stove to make water seem to disappear. The Sun can heat water and make it turn to a gas, too. On a sunny day, you can feel warmth from the Sun on your skin. What do you think happens when the Sun shines on a lake, a river, or even an ocean?

Ocean water evaporates on a warm sunny day. Do you think the water is gone forever?

The ocean is too big and too cold to boil away. But with heat from the Sun, some liquid water molecules get more energy and they start to move faster. Some move fast enough to break out of the liquid and rise into the air as the gas called water vapor. This process is called **evaporation.** Water changes from a liquid to a gas without boiling.

Try this: Fill a plastic cup halfway with water. Use a marker to draw a line at the level of the water. Now, leave the cup in sunlight for a few hours. Did the water level change? Why?

It's Back

You can't see water vapor in the air. But it's there, floating around. Sometimes, water vapor turns back into a liquid.

To get out of the air and become a liquid again, water vapor has to cool down. As it cools, the molecules start to move slower and they get closer together. This process is called **condensation.** Water molecules condense when they touch a surface that's cooler than the air.

When cool water vapor condenses, it can look like it rained outside!

Think about Jack's water glass. Do you need to change your idea about where the water on his glass came from?

You've seen how water can change from one form to another. It can seem to vanish into thin air. It can seem to appear out of thin air. Now, let's talk about what else water can do.

What can water do to some other things?

As a liquid, water can make other things seem to disappear. Try this with an adult: Dump a teaspoon of sugar into a cup of hot water. Stir. Poof! Just like that, the powder is gone. Or is it?

Water is a **solvent.** Some solids, like sugar, **dissolve** in it. The sugar seems to go away. But is it really gone? Let the water cool and then taste it. It will taste sweet. What do you think a cup of water would taste like if you stirred in salt?

Just like good friends, water molecules can stick together.

Why Does Water Bead Up on a Surface?

Next time it rains, stay outside for a while and watch the water. When rain falls on a leaf or a flower, you'll see drops of water form. These are called beads. Why doesn't the rain cover leaves in a flat layer?

The answer brings up another water "power." When they are close to each other, water molecules "stick" to each other a little bit. This property is called **surface tension.**

17

The Water Cycle

What do you think clouds are made of?

Water moves around a lot. On land, the Sun heats the water in oceans, rivers, and lakes. The liquid water turns to water vapor. The water vapor forms clouds. Up in the sky, water vapor cools. Then it falls back to Earth as precipitation— rain, sleet, or snow. There, the **cycle** begins again.

There is only so much water on Earth. You can't get new water or take any of the old water away. Instead, the same water travels around and around. Over and over, it moves from land to sky and back to land. This process is called the water cycle.

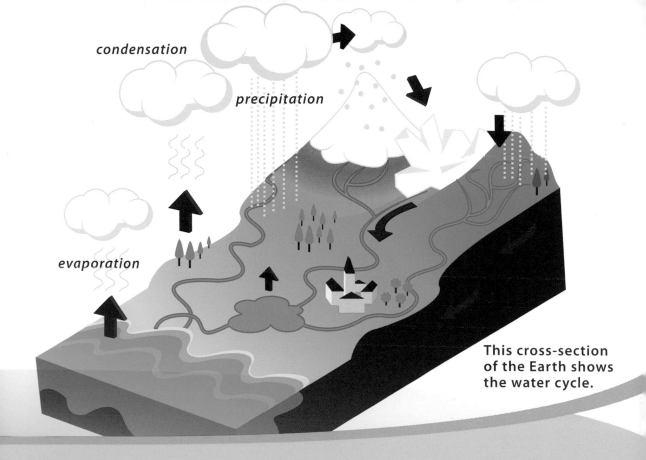

condensation

precipitation

evaporation

This cross-section of the Earth shows the water cycle.

The water cycle is important because people need water to live. Our bodies are made mostly of water. We need it to drink. We need it for growing food. Even the land we live on is shaped by water.

Rivers dig valleys and sculpt mountains. Water also adds a lot of fun to our lives. Without it, you could never swim at the beach. You could never run through sprinklers. And you would never be able to throw a water balloon.

How Does Water Change Land and Rock?

Flowing water looks beautiful...

Water is very strong stuff. A small stream or a trickle of water can seem weak. But over time, that stream or trickle can wear down rock. The faster water moves, the faster it wears the rock away. This process is called **erosion.**

...and it is powerful stuff.

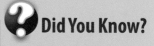

When a river rushes along, erosion picks up speed. The soil wears away. Mud and rocks tumble downstream. Waves hit beaches. They wear down shells and rocks. Sand is made of these tiny bits of shells and rocks. Over time, erosion really changes the way our planet looks.

❓ Did You Know?

The Colorado River carved out the steep sides of the Grand Canyon over millions of years.

The picture may look silly, but the danger of landslides is very real.

Have you ever stood outside in the pouring rain? If so, you've felt the power of water. When there's a lot of it, water can really hurt!

When it rains very hard, water builds up. Flooding can happen. Sometimes, floods push rocks and dirt down hills. The land crumbles. This effect is called a landslide.

How else do you think water can change the way land looks?

Falling rocks can
be a real hazard
on our roadways.

Water sometimes rushes along. But it can also
seem to be very patient. Over time, it slowly shapes
the land. This process is called **weathering.**

Often, water seeps into cracks and holes in
rocks. When the temperature gets very cold, the
water freezes into ice and expands, or spreads out.
(Remember those molecules playing freeze tag?)
As a result, the cracks and holes get bigger. When
the weather gets warmer, the water melts again.
Melting is the name for when water changes from
solid ice back to a liquid. This cycle breaks rocks
into smaller and smaller pieces.

Science at Work

Highway Engineers

You probably travel across roads or highways every day. You might even have noticed what happens to roads after a heavy rain—some flood while others do not. It's the job of special scientists to make sure those roads and highways are safe. These scientists, called highway engineers, have to understand the **slope** of the land, the **texture** of the road surface, and how far drivers can see into the distance. Highway engineers also need to understand how roads react to heavy rainfall. Without highway engineers, our roads and highways could be dangerous surfaces to travel on.

Highway engineers work hard to be sure our roads are safe to travel on.

Erosion on the Shoreline: Sinking Beaches

Stilts keep these buildings out of the waves, to protect them from damage.

Playing in ocean waves can be loads of fun. But ocean waves are powerful. Their power causes a lot of erosion. When strong waves hit a beach, they wear away rocks and sand. Over time, the waves can creep farther up on shore. They get closer and closer to buildings. If waves crash into buildings, they cause lots of damage.

Scientists study ocean shorelines. They want to understand how storms and weather patterns cause erosion. Builders also need to know about erosion. That helps them decide how close to the ocean it is safe to build. Do you think it's safe to put buildings near ocean beaches? What is a safe distance from the ocean's edge?

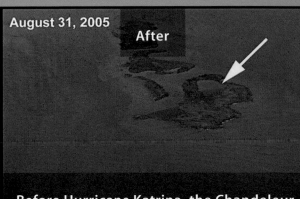

Before Hurricane Katrina, the Chandeleur Islands helped to protect Louisiana from erosion. The storm forever changed the way they look. Now they don't protect the coastline the way they once did. See how much less land is in the photo at right than there is on the photo at left.

Connecting to History

Hurricane Katrina

When Hurricane Katrina hit the U.S. Gulf Coast in 2005, it caused major beach erosion. The Chandeleur Islands, off the Louisiana coast, were almost completely washed away. These islands were barrier islands. Before the hurricane, they stopped strong storms and waves from causing floods on the mainland. Sometimes, barrier islands can come back after hurricanes. Sand might move in and build them back up. But so far, the Chandeleur Islands have not been built back up. Without them, the mainland is in more danger of losing land to erosion.

Now can you help Jack solve the mystery of the wet glass?

Let's return to Jack's glass of ice water. The glass is wet on the outside. Why?

First, Jack should check to see if the glass is leaking. Are there any cracks or holes? If so, the glass is probably wet in just one place. So, what if there are no cracks and the whole glass is wet? Where could the water be coming from?

The answer is condensation. Water vapor in the air touched the cold surface of the glass. The molecules in the gas got closer together when they cooled on the glass, and they turned into liquid.

What happened to the two glasses you put on the table? Write down what you saw.

28   How does condensation explain what happened?

Now that you're a water expert, try these experiments.

- Place an empty glass outside in the morning. Leave it there for one day and one night. The next day, check the glass in the early morning and in the evening. Did you see condensation on the glass? If so, when? Why did condensation occur at that time? If you did not see condensation, explain why not.

- On another day, try this: Place wet clothes on a clothesline. Did they dry? If so, why? If not, what would need to happen for them to dry?

- Finally, breathe on a mirror. What happened? Why do you think it happened?

Water's power can seem like magic. But, now you know that there are simple ways to explain these science "tricks."

GLOSSARY

boiling: changing from a liquid to a gas.

condensation: the process by which water vapor changes into liquid droplets that collect on a cold surface.

cycle: events that happen over and over again in the same order.

dissolve: to mix a solid substance into a liquid substance.

erosion: the wearing away of rocks and soil.

evaporation: a process of water changing from a liquid to a gas.

freezing: changing from a liquid to a solid.

gas: the state of a substance in which it spreads out into all available space.

liquid: the state of a substance in which it takes the shape of the container or area it occupies.

melting: changing from a solid to a liquid.

molecules: little bits of a substance, much smaller than a drop.

slope: slant or incline downward or upward.

solid: the state of a substance that has a definite shape.

solvent: a substance that helps other substances mix in, or dissolve.

surface tension: the ability of water to stick to itself.

texture: how an object or material feels. For example, sandpaper has a rough texture.

water vapor: the gas form of water.

weathering: a process in which rocks are broken down in place, often caused by water.

FURTHER READING

Erosion, by Joelle Riley. Lerner Classroom, 2007.

One Well: The Story of Water on Earth, by Rochelle Strauss. Kids Can Press, 2007.

The Water Cycle, by Bobbie Kalman. Crabtree Publishing Co., 2009.

The Water Cycle, www.kidzone.ws/water

ADDITIONAL NOTES

The page references below provide answers to questions asked throughout the book. Questions whose answers will vary are not addressed.

Page 8: Water changes from a liquid to a gas when it boils.

Page 14: When the sun shines on a body of water, it warms it. Yes, the water level changes because of evaporation.

Page 16: The water would taste salty.

Page 26: A safe distance from the ocean's edge would be far away from any erosion that might happen during the very worst storms.

Page 28: Water leaves the vapor in the warm air and condenses into liquid when it cools on the glass of cold water.